Elemar Kleber Favreto
Rafael P. Ferreira Dias

Education and Teaching in Brazil and the State of Roraima

Elemar Kleber Favreto
Rafael P. Ferreira Dias

Education and Teaching in Brazil and the State of Roraima

Philosophical Contributions to Citizen Education

ScienciaScripts

Publisher:
Sciencia Scripts
is a trademark of
Dodo Books Indian Ocean Ltd. and OmniScriptum S.R.L publishing group

120 High Road, East Finchley, London, N2 9ED, United Kingdom
Str. Armeneasca 28/1, office 1, Chisinau MD-2012, Republic of Moldova, Europe
Printed at: see last page
ISBN: 978-620-7-69658-1

SUMMARY

PRESENTATION

Philosophy works with concepts, it creates concepts, it searches for the foundation of things in the world. It differs from common sense in that it has this commitment to foundations; it differs from art in that it seeks an expression that goes beyond sensation and aesthetic enjoyment; it also differs from science in that it doesn't operate with something already founded, that is, it doesn't take a theory or set of theories as truth, even if it's provisional; on the contrary, it opens up the field to various perspectives of truth. However, common sense, art and science provide the philosopher with the necessary conditions for a new conceptual creation. In this way, philosophy is a field open to multidisciplinary discussion, as it uses knowledge in general to prompt its investigations and reflections. Knowledge, in this way, is broader than a discipline, a "little box" in which we can encapsulate a spectrum of human reason, which is why Philosophy is able to engage in this dialogue with the different perspectives of man and the world.

The principles that form the basis of our society are rooted in philosophical foundations that permeate the entire history of humanity. This shows how philosophy plays an important role in shaping our own subjectivity and our sense of community. Thus, if we hope for a change in society, this change must first take place in the individual, making them understand their relationship with others and with the world. Philosophy, in this sense, can help discover some paths to this understanding, showing that its teaching is of paramount importance so that the new generations can begin a process of change in the social reality of Brazil and the world.

This publication is a collection of texts produced by teachers and students of the *Lato Sensu* Post-Graduation in Fundamentals of Philosophy at the State University of Roraima (UERR), the result of their research into various areas of knowledge which, in one way or another, give rise to philosophical reflection. The main theme addressed here, however, is teaching and its relationship with philosophy. Divided into four chapters, this book seeks to discuss, from the point of view of each of its authors, the role of philosophy in basic education, as well as in the formation of subjectivity, citizenship and society itself.

We are sure that this book can serve as a guide for future reflections and debates by researchers in the field of philosophy teaching, as well as an aid for undergraduate and postgraduate students interested in undertaking a philosophical and multidisciplinary discussion within universities.

We would like to thank the professors and students of the Postgraduate Program in Fundamentals of Philosophy at UERR, who helped to produce this work, especially the authors of the book. We would also like to thank the State University of Roraima and Novas Edipoes Academicas for their support in developing this project.

Elemar Kleber Favreto

Professor of Philosophy and Vice-Rector of the State University of Roraima

CHAPTER I
LIFE AND CULTURE: THE CHALLENGES OF EDUCATION FOR THE NEW MILLENNIUM

Renata Viana Serafim Rafael Parente Ferreira Dias

INITIAL CONSIDERATIONS

When we reflect on pedagogical issues, a number of teaching methodologies immediately come to mind, and these, in turn, present different ways of thinking about and doing education. In Rubem Alves' view, pedagogical ideas and practices are often at odds with the essence, the fundamentals and the foundations of education. Aiming to redirect the vectors of the educational system, Rubem Alves proposes a form of learning based on experiences and content linked to life itself. More than that, the crux of education is to get *students to enjoy knowledge.* In this sense, the knowledge generated in schools must, in some way, participate in and dialog with the outside world, in other words, with the students' social and cultural context. Ready-made answers and mechanical formulas should be avoided, and it is up to the educator to foster in students a desire for the new, the unusual, in other words, the student himself should generate knowledge from himself, from his own analysis. This simple method is capable of awakening the joy and pleasure of knowledge, because instead of receiving it ready-made, the student needs to discover it, and this is the magic of teaching.

After this brief prelude, we will analyze an analogy by Rubem Alves, who compares the educator to the cook. The cook, by the smell, appearance and taste of his food, always makes it desirable, and the educator, in the same way, will present the subject by making it "appetizing" for the students:

> Without hunger, the body refuses to eat. Overstuffed, it vomits. Every learning experience begins with an emotional experience. It is hunger that sets the thinking apparatus in motion. Thought is born out of affection; hunger is born out of the desire to eat. Do not confuse affection with kisses and cuddles. Affection, from the Latin *affetare,* means to go after. Affection is the movement of the soul in search of the object of its hunger. It's Platonian *eros,* the hunger that makes the soul fly in search of the dreamed-of fruit (ALVES, 2004, p. 20).

"The true cook is the one who knows the art of producing hunger" (ALVES

2004, p. 20). Similarly, we can see that the aesthetic dimension of education, based on Rubem Alves' reflections, refers to the *art of teaching, of* provoking "hunger" or the passionate desire for knowledge in the heart of the student.

The "hunger" or "affection" for knowledge must be constantly stimulated by educators. To this end, students need to get used to coming up with creative solutions to problems formulated in class, based on this pedagogy. Instead of coming up with a ready-made answer, the teacher suggests alternative channels, so that the student doesn't passively receive knowledge, but rather searches within himself, with deep reflection, for the answers to the questions raised. On this point, Rubem Alves points out that:

> [...] if the desire is satisfied, the thinking machine doesn't think. So if the wish is fulfilled, the thought doesn't happen. The easiest way to abort thought is to fulfill the desire. This is the sin of many parents and teachers who teach answers before there have been questions (ALVES, 2004, p. 21)

The big question in relation to thinking concerns what happens in the classroom, because the answers are already ready before the questions are asked, and the provocation of curiosity in the student doesn't occur precisely because they aren't led to think. "Curiosity is an itch in the ideas" (ALVES, 2004, p. 8).

A taste for the unknown, for the unusual, for "what can be different" is the sure-fire path towards aesthetic pleasure applied to education. Uncertainties are capable of taking students out of their comfort zone, actively reallocating them in the process of producing knowledge. In this sense, the student feels part of knowledge, inserted into a dimension of learning that frees them from the prison of passivity. Once the drama of "intellectual passivity" has been overcome, the possibility arises of critical questioning, of stimulating questions, which lead us into the sea of the unknown:

> Thought is like an eagle that only flies in the empty spaces of the unknown. Thinking is flying over what you don't know. There is nothing more fatal to teaching than the right answers. That's why schools exist: not to teach answers, but to teach questions. Answers allow us to walk on solid ground. But only questions allow us to enter the sea of the unknown (ALVES, 1994, p. 67).

When a student is asked a question in the classroom by the teacher, a wave of curiosity immediately takes hold of him, stimulating him to search within himself for the solution to the problem presented. The same happens with the philosopher when he finds something in the world that provokes his curiosity, he starts thinking in search of answers, but he doesn't find them, only more questions.

In this sense, Alves points out that knowledge, in order to be fully absorbed by the student, must first be desired. Desire, therefore, is a prerequisite for knowledge:

> It's not something I made up. It was taught to me. I didn't have to think about it. I liked it. It went into memory. This is the fundamental rule of this computer that lives in the human body: only what is the object of desire goes into memory. The teacher's primary task: to seduce the student so that he desires and, desiring, learns. And knowledge is memorized by heart - etymologically in the heart - waiting for the desire key to call it back from its place of oblivion (ALVES, 1994, p. 70).

For Rubem Alves, there is an aesthetic dimension to education, which is concerned with the harmony and balance of the elements involved. Throughout his texts, by comparing the educator to the cook, as already mentioned, he questions the very act of "teaching", the educator's task par excellence, but another question immediately arises: "Teaching what?". Let's look at his answer: "[...] the master teaches happiness" (ALVES, 1994, p. 9). Happiness is linked to the desire to know, to the pleasure of knowledge itself, this is his conclusion, as we can see in the following quote:

> [...] isn't what you teach a delight for the soul? If it wasn't, you shouldn't teach. And if it is, then those who receive it, your students, must feel the same pleasure as you do. If this doesn't happen, you will have failed in your mission, like the cook who wanted to offer pleasure, but the food came out salty and burnt. [...] The master is born from the exuberance of happiness. And that's why, when asked about their profession, teachers should have the courage to give the absurd answer: "I am a shepherd of joy" ... But, of course, only their students will be able to attest to the truth of their statement (ALVES, 1994, p. 10).

Therefore, if the educator doesn't provoke the students' curiosity, if he doesn't enjoy teaching, he won't succeed. The student's happiness comes from the interaction between pleasure and knowledge, both of which must go hand in hand. In this sense, aesthetic pleasure is the result of the knowledge transmitted by the teacher, who, in turn, must constantly provoke the "hunger of curiosity" in the students, so that they can rethink the world from their own conceptions, re-signified by this new teaching-learning methodology.

The idea of the "construction of the world" linked to the educational process is one of the important points that also deserves to be highlighted in this chapter. In the following paragraphs, we will delve deeper into this fundamental relationship between education, man and culture.

THE CONSTRUCTION OF MAN THROUGH CULTURE AND THE ROLE OF EDUCATION

The term "culture", of Latin origin, means to *cultivate*. The relationship between man and culture involves the cultivation of what man has built and is building, with an emphasis on his construction of the world. On this point, Duarte (1995, p. 50) points out:

> [...] man, who has transformed this rudimentary scheme into a system of values and meanings, seeks to modify the environment by building the world. Unlike animals, the environment must adapt to man; it must be organized on the basis of his values and meanings. And this means the creation of culture. The physical environment, raw and governed by natural forces, to which the animal adjusts, can be called nature. This, taken by man and modified according to his needs, becomes culture. The very act of ordering and structuring the perceived world through symbols is already the creation of culture. Therefore, man and culture are inextricably linked: there is only culture through man, and man only exists through culture.

From a philosophical point of view, culture manifests itself through the way man relates to himself, to other men and to nature itself. The way they draw up their laws, build their houses, establish customs and sanctions, feed and educate their children, all of these constitute the values created by human beings and conventionally accepted by the entire social spectrum.

Duarte (1995, p. 53) states that the patterns related to the habits and customs of a people represent the expression of local feelings and idiosyncrasies, each with its own specificities and characteristics:

> Thus, culture is the expression of that characteristic pattern of feeling that distinguishes one people from another, in the pattern of their actions and in the things involved in their actions, or in other words , in their things, specifically. Acts generally have a purpose, and things are useful, that is, they serve a purpose ; but both acts and artifacts have a purpose. They go beyond practical needs, such as taking on a formal character, which is not effective but expressive. [...] In short: by building culture, man realizes his values, and aesthetic values, rhythm and harmony, are fundamental to order, to meaning.

Leaving the philosophical sphere and entering the anthropological view, Brandao (1990) points out that cultural identity is not constructed in a singular, exclusive way, as it is progressively produced. The fact is that the terms "identity" and "social" lead, in a reciprocal way, to the sense of a "self", necessarily constituted through social interactions. Therefore, in the anthropological sphere, an individual's identity is closely linked to their participation in a cultural scene, and the two are irremediably connected. In this sense, the dynamics of social relationships have no meaning unless they are linked to the individual themselves, as the main axis of these manifestations.

From a sociological point of view, Edgar Morin sees "identity" in a universal way. For him, human identity is what makes us human, what unites us as human beings, and this is an issue that cannot be ignored by planetary education. On this point, Morin (2003, p. 98) clarifies:

> The mission of education for the planetary era is to strengthen the conditions of possibility for the emergence of a world-society made up of protagonist citizens who are consciously and critically committed to building a planetary civilization.

Planetary education therefore concerns the relationship not only between the disciplinary contents of different areas, but also between the individual, society and nature; body, mind and emotions, in other words, "[...] Planetary education must provide a mundology of everyday life" (MORIN, 2003, p. 99).

As individuals of the same species, we have the same needs. At the same time, we are diverse in culture, in the organization of societies, races, languages, etc. Education must foster understanding, mutual agreement between nations, respect for cultural differences and beware of prejudiced judgments. These should be the guiding principles of a serious pedagogy committed to the common good, to the "world-society".

Let's look at Morin's opinion (2003, p. 64):

> Education must reinforce respect for cultures and understand that they are imperfect in themselves, the image of the human being. All cultures, like ours, are a mixture of superstitions, fictions, fixations, accumulated and uncriticized knowledge, gross errors and profound truths, but this mixture is not discernible at first glance and we must be careful not to classify ancient knowledge as superstitions, like, for example, the ways in which maize is prepared in Mexico, which for a long time anthropologists attributed to magical beliefs, until it was discovered that they allowed the body to assimilate lysine, a nutritious substance that for a long time was its only food. Thus, what seemed "irrational" responded to a vital rationality.

This universal identity, for Morin, will be given through a planetary education, so that we can protect ourselves as a species, as social beings and as individuals.

This approach reveals a close relationship between cultural identity and education, since it is through education that a "cultural vision of the world" becomes possible. On this point, Duarte (1995, p. 59) adds:

> In broad terms, it can be understood as a process through which individuals acquire their cultural personality. In other words: to be educated is first of all to acquire the worldview of the culture to which one belongs; to be educated is to learn the values and feelings that structure the community in which we live.

Educating means allowing the individual to choose a meaning to guide their existence. Symbolisations are only grasped to the extent that they connect with life experience. Therefore, to educate is to re-signify our worldview.

Thus, education does not create its own meanings out of thin air, because it is necessary to know what exists in culture in order to integrate into it and thus lead the individual to understand it, creating their own meaning. In this way, only an education geared towards the student's concrete reality can contribute to a more effective world view, as Duarte (1995, p. 74) observes:

> The big problem with education that doesn't talk about a concrete reality, that doesn't refer the concepts transmitted to the world around the students, is that it doesn't produce learning. It only produces individuals who "memorize" concepts and abstractions in order to use them the only time they might be useful to them. What school demands is just the verbose repetition of countless insignificant concepts.

Education can and must play a vital role in any society. However, in order to take on this social role, it can never be detached from the student's concrete reality. In other words, it is from culture that the human world is built, with its meanings and values that lead to and emphasize its existence as a being different from other animals, precisely because we are rational and, consequently, endowed with language. Everything that man builds is, in fact, to express his values.

FINAL CONSIDERATIONS

For Rubem Alves, education goes beyond tests, assessments and entrance exams. The rigor of method and technique is replaced by a *pedagogy of passion, of the* pleasure of getting to know the reality that surrounds us. His proposal is to awaken in the student the fascination, the magic of knowledge, because in this way knowledge becomes a delight for the senses. The utilitarian aims of education, i.e. making school a mere stepping stone to the job market, are not the best way to stimulate the *desire for wisdom.* In this way, the educator's great challenge is to awaken the student's passion and burning desire for knowledge.

Connected to the ideas of Rubem Alves, we also carried out a study on the construction of the human world through culture. In fact, as has already been shown, man is a sociable being, endowed with rational and linguistic structures that allow him to establish interactions with other living beings. With the simple act of verbalizing, we are able to understand each other and establish habits and customs that are conventionally accepted by the social group; this is how the culture of a people and a region is gradually formed.

Unquestionably, education, especially as formulated by Rubem Alves, is of vital importance for the full development of culture. Throughout this chapter we have tried to demonstrate that a well-educated society, with solid pedagogical principles, can be decisive in producing healthy cultural habits, based on noble ideals such as justice, respect and fraternity. This is the great challenge facing the educational process in the coming millennia.

REFERENCES

ABBAGNANO, Nicola. **Dictionary of Philosophy**. Sao Paulo: WMF Martins Fontes, 2012.

ALVES, Rubem. **Philosophy of science:** introduction to the game and its rules. Sao Paulo: Ed. Brasiliense, 1981.

. **Conversations with those who like to teach.** Sao Paulo: Ed. Cortez, 1980.

. **The joy of teaching.** Sao Paulo: Ed. Ars Poetica LTDA, 1994.

. **The desire to teach and the art of learning.** Campinas, Ed. Educar, 2004.

BRANDAO, Carlos: **Identity and ethnicity:** construction of the person and cultural resistance. Sao Paulo: Brasiliense, 1990.

DUARTE JUNIOR, Joao Francisco. **Aesthetic Foundations of Education.** Campinas, SP: Papirus, 1995.

MORIN, Edgar. **Educating in the planetary age:** complex thinking as a learning method in human error and uncertainty. Sao Paulo: Cortez, 2003.

CHAPTER II

THE PHILOSOPHY TEACHER AND THE TEACHING OF PHILOSOPHY IN BRAZIL

Neusa Wigner Matte Elemar Kleber Favreto

INITIAL CONSIDERATIONS

Nowadays, with the current cultural situation (marked by consumerism and the strong presence of the media, which have limited the educational process), we seek what is useful, what immediately meets our needs, or rather, the needs required for us to be part of this world and this culture. Perhaps this is the biggest challenge, because in this environment, the question that society usually asks is: what is philosophy for? What is the importance of this subject in the formative process of our teenagers?

These questions pose one of the great problems facing education today: How can we think about philosophy in the fast-paced world of information in which we live today?

Brazilian secondary schools have Philosophy as part of their curriculum. However, this was not always the case, as it was absent from the curriculum for many years. It was absent, for example, for much of the period of the military regime, when Law No. 7.044 of 1982 made it optional in public and private schools, without, however, guaranteeing its presence in the curriculum, especially in public education, which, for the most part, chose not to include it as a subject[1] . It was only in 2008 that Philosophy was once again included as a compulsory subject in the secondary school curricula of Brazilian public schools, with the advent of Law No. 11.683. This compulsory teaching of Philosophy took place at a time of rapid transformation in contemporary society, where major technological advances have had a direct impact on society's behavior; since the means of communication end up directly affecting the school, increasing the challenges of making it a democratic, effective and accessible achievement for all, without losing its depth.

With the inclusion of Philosophy, the aim was to resolve the ambiguity in the Law of Guidelines and Bases of National Education (LDB), which, in its article 36,

---

[1] Philosophy began to be taught again in 1985, when the subject was introduced in secondary school teaching courses, usually in private schools run by churchmen.

paragraph 1, item III, states that "[...] all students must, at the end of Secondary Education, demonstrate, in addition to other skills, mastery of the knowledge of Philosophy, necessary for the exercise of citizenship".

Some important factors that we intend to address and that we believe are necessary for the development of skills for teaching philosophy are those that concern the planning and diversification of lessons, or even those that contemplate the skills of mastering philosophical language, enabling high school students and teachers to reflect on the conditions for teaching content related to this subject, as well as its role today.

It is necessary to bring up for discussion some questions that could guide the teaching of philosophy in high school. Some of these questions can be found in the article *Philosopher versus Philosophy Teacher,* by Julio Cesar Gongalves and Divino Jose da Silva, which are: Is it possible to teach Philosophy? How should it be taught? What has been the training of teachers working in the subject? Is the time offered for classroom discussions sufficient for productive reflection? With regard to teaching materials, have they found this support in educational institutions?

Thinking about philosophy teaching that is committed to a philosophical experience is the proposal for the return of philosophy to secondary education. However, this will not be possible if teacher training is not in line with the demands of philosophizing and if the time offered for classroom discussions is insufficient for more productive reflection. Thus, the teaching of philosophy needs to be thought of as an experience for students, since only in this way would it be taken as a discipline that seeks to think the unthinkable (philosophizing), in the sense of questioning what is not usually questioned. Here we can point to another question: how to consolidate this demand of situations facing philosophy teaching?

In this chapter, therefore, we will try to briefly address the conditions of the Philosophy teaching in Brazil, in a historical sketch of Brazilian schools , and the current conditions of the subject in Secondary Education , as well as the training of the
teacher who works in the area. This could guide us towards a broader reflection on the philosophy curriculum and the very dimension of the compulsory nature of philosophical knowledge in secondary education, as pointed out in the reformulation of basic education.

A BRIEF HISTORY OF PHILOSOPHY TEACHING IN BRAZIL

We face many challenges in teaching philosophy today, as we live in what Alain Touraine and Daniel Bell (in the late 1960s and early 1970s) called the "information society"; a society that is much more concerned with the "virtual space" of the image than with the transparency and veracity of the information it disseminates. Philosophy, however, has the following main guidelines: working with concepts (through reading and reflecting on philosophical texts), developing critical thinking (by linking human problems with their philosophical history) and also using non-philosophical texts (literature, newspaper reports, magazines, films, music, poetry, artwork, etc.) to help with conceptual creation. In the classroom, this helps students to make connections between the text/context and the problems that surround it, making philosophical reflection meaningful for them.

In this sense, there is a difficulty, since philosophy classes end up having to compete for space, in addition to common sense and the sciences (which they usually do), with the technological means that enable this virtual discussion in the classroom (laptops, tablets, smartphones, etc.). Thus, we need to better understand the skills that secondary education should (or ought to) provide students with, so we can look to the LDB itself (Law no. 9394/96, art. 35) to explain some of the purposes that this level of education has and tries to provide as a goal for students:

> The aims of secondary education are, in addition to basic preparation for work and citizenship, the development of the student as a human being, including ethical formation and the development of intellectual autonomy and critical thinking (item III) and the understanding of the scientific and technological foundations of production processes, relating theory to practice in the teaching of each subject (item IV).

These aims should govern all high school subjects, but we realize that this is not the case. Even more so when important subjects such as Philosophy and Sociology have been left out of the curriculum for so long.

When we look at the history of philosophy teaching in Brazil, for example, we realize that it was not a constant in Brazilian public schools. In colonial Brazil, education was in the hands of the Jesuits and Philosophy was linked to Religious Education. When the Jesuits were expelled, education was left in the hands of laypeople who followed the Jesuit path because they had received it. Philosophy began to be separated from religious education in the middle of the 18th century and became a subject. In 1911, philosophy was removed from the curriculum for the first time, when it was replaced by civics and general law. This absence lasted until 1915, with Maximilian's reform, when philosophy returned to the curriculum, but on an optional basis (JHOANIA, 2011).

In the period between 1925, with the Joao Luiz Alves Reform, and 1961, with the first LDB, it was present in the school curriculum as compulsory. From 1961, it returned to optional *status,* being replaced by other subjects in 1971, after the military coup, with Law No. 5.692/71, remaining permanently absent until the mid-1980s, when Law No. 7.044 of 1982 made it optional again in public and private schools. This return, however, did not guarantee its presence in the curriculum, especially in public schools, the vast majority of which chose not to include this subject in the curriculum, as it would reduce the workload of other subjects.

In changes to the National Education Guidelines and Bases Law (LDB), Law No. 9.394 of 1996, it was pointed out that it included in its text that all secondary school students should leave school having mastered knowledge of Philosophy and Sociology, which were equally necessary for the exercise of citizenship. This was a breakthrough, as it once again opened up the possibility of Philosophy being present at this level of education. However, the new LDB did not stipulate how this content should be taught, opening up the possibility of it being taught in other subjects in secondary education. This, therefore, did not necessarily lead to Philosophy returning to schools as a subject. It was only in 2008 that Philosophy was once again included as a compulsory subject in the secondary school curricula of Brazilian schools, with the advent of Law No. 11.683/2008.

This was the journey of the Philosophy subject through Brazilian education. We realized that for a long time Philosophy was left out of the curriculum, causing discontinuity in its teaching, but also a unity of teachers of the subject through the struggle for its return to Brazilian education.

PHILOSOPHICAL OPERATION IN SECONDARY EDUCATION AND THE PROBLEM OF TECHNOLOGY

Taking into account the need to teach philosophy in Brazilian high schools, but also because they are part of a society that is constantly changing (philosophy is older than the school itself), according to Rodrigo Pelloso Gelamo (2006, p. 9), in his article *The Problem of Experience in Philosophy Teaching:*

> Although philosophy is older than the university, it only found a privileged place in it in the Middle Ages and, at the same time, we are witnessing its rejection. We believe that this rejection, this decline of philosophy, is the result of a series of problems ranging from poorly designed curricular proposals to an ideology that aims to exalt technological knowledge.

In a technologically equipped world, where we need to master this skill in order to participate in a competitive market, our young people are being pushed into the job market at an increasingly early age, justified by the way in which today's society accumulates capital. Marilena Chaui (1992, p. 56-57) points this out very well in her article *What is it to be an educator today? From art to citizenship: the death of the educator.*

> We live in a world dominated by what the dominant ideology has come to call 'technological progress'. The result of the physical and psychological exploitation of thousands of men, women and children, the domestication of their bodies and spirits by a fragmented process devoid of meaning, the reduction of subjects to the condition of socio-economic objects, manipulable politically and by the structures of bureaucratic-administrative organization, 'progress' hijacks personal identity, social responsibility, political direction and the right to produce culture for all non-dominants.

The question that can be raised from these two quotes is: how can we think for ourselves if what is worth teaching today is not the cultivation of thought, culture or the person, but "knowledge" that puts students directly into the job market?

It is clear that reflection on the knowledge accumulated by man is often excluded from school curricula, or treated, as Gelamo says, as "perfumery". Understanding how truth and knowledge have developed throughout the history of philosophy is essential if we are to reflect on the need for their inclusion in school curricula. Thus, according to Larrosa, the problem of experience and true knowledge can be seen as far back as Greek thought, which understood practical experience as inferior to knowledge aimed at contemplation:

> In classical philosophy, experience was understood as an inferior mode of knowledge, perhaps necessary as a starting point, but not of true knowledge, or even, in some classical authors, experience was an obstacle to true knowledge, to true science (LARROSA 2004 *apud* GELAMO, 2006, p. 10).

For Plato, for example, experience only allowed access to the corporeal world, the world of imperfect forms, uncertainty, belief and opinion. According to him, experience would not provide us with a correct way of doing philosophy, making experience a problem for true knowledge, which would only be possible through the contemplation of what is immutable and exquisite, the world of ideas.

The incorporation of scientific discoveries into the production process in the capitalist world, however, demands practical support from man, making practical knowledge what directs us to true knowledge, scientific knowledge. This goes against the Greek, and especially Platonist, view of what true knowledge is. From the point of view of technology and science, therefore, philosophical thinking is no longer necessary. Taking into account the problem of teaching in the current pedagogical context, two currents stand out:

> [...] on the one hand, the critical strand, which focuses on the discussion of theory and practice, aiming for a reflexive praxis in the educational process; and, on the other, the scientific-educational strand, which sees education as an applied science, whose objective is to seek methods and techniques for teaching, based on slogans such as: efficiency, evaluation, productivity and so on. In this context, experience is a word whose meaning makes no sense: either because it is constituted as "knowledge" whose content is the result of alienation - since the link between theory and practice is not established on a secure basis - which culminates in an emancipatory praxis, or because it is not based on scientific criteria of proven value and is considered just an opinion or common sense (LARROSA, 2004; BARCENA, 2005, *apud* GELAMO, 2006, p. 11).

It can be said that today practically all the knowledge accumulated by humanity is available to anyone who owns a computer, a tablet or a computer. smartphone and access to an internet service provider. nternet information has become a challenge for educators, and even more so for humanities subjects, which require individuals to be concerned about the quality of this information, as well as their criticality, i.e. they need to reflect on the information. As such, intellectual emancipation is much harder to achieve today, so the idea that "anyone can teach", even what they don't know, is prevalent, especially if they act according to the mechanisms provided by the information industry. Thus, both teaching and learning become superficial in this world where Information and Communication Technologies (ICTs) end up taking precedence over reflective classroom practice. This is why updating teachers is fundamental to transforming pedagogical practice.

The complexity of teaching philosophy in secondary schools in Brazil is a challenge for the Humanities area, since in addition to the widespread use of ICT, which has a lot of information and often little reflective content, students find themselves at the crossroads of not understanding the educational system and not even recognizing themselves within this system, as a thinking subject and facilitator of reflection to change the social reality of their students.

In order for us to find ways of seeking an emancipation of thought, we need to find instruments that allow us to teach through a reflective experience; in other words, we educators need to find ways of looking for a relationship between philosophical reflection and the problems that surround us in our students' daily lives, in their technological practice (which uses ICTs to discover the world). In view of this, we contemplate the idea that there is no single method for learning or teaching philosophy, and therefore recognize that it is necessary to make philosophy an experience for both the student and the teacher. In this way, we share the thinking of Renata Aspis and Silvio Gallo, who, in their *book Teaching Philosophy: a book for teachers,* point out that we must understand:

> [...] that learning is a kind of event, beyond our control, does not in any way mean that teaching is done at random. Teachers need to equip themselves with a repertoire, build classroom strategies, define their objectives and outline courses of action [...] (ASPIS; GALLO, 2009, p. 69).

Philosophers, for example, each in their own time, have created their own methods for constructing philosophical thought, always seeking to regulate, never to randomize. In this way, we consider the current preoccupation with the teaching of philosophy to be legitimate, since it generates various reflections on how we can think about philosophy and how we can teach it in such a way that knowledge can once again build a practical and experimental framework, capable of sustaining the weight of its theories and the greatness of its history. In order to do this, we need to reflect on the fact that there is still no tradition of teaching philosophy in Brazilian schools and, furthermore, there is still a great deal of distrust, on the part of society in general, of its importance for teaching, since it stems from an abstract study that is not aimed at immediate application, as today's technological world wants.

TEACHING AND TRAINING PHILOSOPHY TEACHERS

It is often said that the role of the philosophy teacher is to put students in touch with the classic authors of the history of philosophy, or with the great philosophical themes. This conception seems a little outdated in a globalized age, where ICT ends up training and informing much more than the teacher. Although it may seem backward for current Brazilian education, the teacher should still prioritize some aspects of this conception in the classroom, since the essence of philosophical work itself is made up of research and conceptual creation; that is, there is only Philosophy to the extent that concepts are created, which can only arise from research within the History of Philosophy. The education of secondary school pupils should therefore prioritize some general guidelines on how philosophy works, so that students can have contact with this form of knowledge, which often contrasts with their reality. However, we can't expect high school students to create innovative concepts within Philosophy, but what is important is that we can provide students with the perspective that is proper to this type of knowledge, which can't be found in any other subject. Thus, philosophy classes thought of as philosophical experiences must take into account the philosophy teacher's own philosophical experience, making him or her a mediator of the knowledge accumulated within the History of Philosophy.

The big problem with Brazilian education, however, especially secondary education, is that its curriculum is built exclusively for "entrance exam training", although in recent years a reformulation of the curriculum has been sought with the "Movement for a Common Curriculum Base", which, however, ends up prioritizing certain knowledge even more, precisely because part of the curriculum is compulsory for the whole country. Classroom work in high school, therefore, prioritizes the content that will be present in the entrance exams of Brazilian universities. In this sense, as Philosophy is a compulsory subject, it also has compulsory content, which students must master by the end of secondary school.

We need to think of a way to overcome this curricular model, since, according to Franklin Leopoldo e Silva, in his *article History of Philosophy: Center or Reference?* It reminds us of the idea of training, while the:

> [...] the appropriate combination of the acquisition of technical skills in preparation and identification, on the one hand, and the recognition of the genesis and foundation of the procedures applied [...]. The aim is to make the transmission of knowledge as close as possible to a reproduction of discovery, of knowing in the dynamic sense (SILVA, 1992, p. 159).

As well as trying to overcome the problems of the curriculum, a problem faced by all secondary school teachers, the subject of Philosophy faces two other major problems: firstly, the poor training of Philosophy graduates; and secondly, the divergence between philosophical research and Philosophy teaching.

Philosophy degree courses in Brazil are very deficient in terms of pedagogy, since many students who graduate with a degree in Philosophy do not have sufficient resources to enter a secondary school classroom. The issue is that philosophy degrees generally don't train students to be philosophy teachers, but rather philosophy researchers. What's more, in general, degree courses are not viewed favorably by the vast majority of the population, who are looking for courses in more technical areas, as well as research areas:

> A quick look at the emergence of teacher training courses to work at secondary level in Brazil points to their historical discredit in relation to research training, and the classification of such courses as second-rate in the general context of universities. Compared to other higher education courses, which train liberal professionals and researchers, degree courses are among those with the lowest number of candidates per place on the entrance exam, with lower rates of success (TOMAZETTI, 2002, p. 21).

In philosophy courses, this seems to get worse, as many undergraduates end up leaving the course without adequate teaching training, so that they either become disillusioned with the teaching profession, taking their teachers as a model, or become frustrated with secondary education, as they don't know or discuss the real situation of this level of education properly. The vast majority of secondary school teachers end up becoming discouraged during their first few years on the job. Silvio Gallo and Walter Kohan, in their article *Critique of some commonplaces when thinking about Philosophy in Secondary Education,* discuss these issues further:

> Our higher education philosophy courses, with honorable exceptions, do not nurture educators and discourage the educational dimension of philosophy. At the same time, they promote a division of labor that is highly detrimental to philosophy itself: one would be the logical nature of the production of philosophical knowledge, and the other would be the logic of the circulation of philosophical knowledge. This distinction prevents us from understanding the intrinsically educational logic of philosophy, which is part of it, throughout its history, in its texts, in its practice (GALLO; KOHAN. 2000, p. 181).

Reflections on teacher training for secondary education point to some important questions that will not be answered in this chapter, such as: what can be considered good teacher training? How do philosophy degrees position themselves with regard to teaching and schools? How prestigious is the philosophy teacher in society?

These issues will require a broader reflection and should be part of the initial and continuing training courses for philosophy teachers in Brazil.

Thus, the intention of this chapter is to raise this discussion, seeking to further broaden the teacher's view of the Brazilian school and education.

FINAL CONSIDERATIONS

The important role of contributing to the education of young people in the face of all contemporary problems makes philosophy a subject that requires greater attention in secondary schools. The philosophical experience in secondary school implies a provocation: getting young people out of their comfort zones so that, through philosophy, they can overturn some of their certainties, provoking doubts about the things that surround them. Every philosophy lesson should exert the power to provoke in the other a movement of deconstruction and reconstruction of concepts, that is, to cause in the other a difference, a form of transformation, as well as a means for the student to be able to search for themselves, become critical of themselves and, with this, learn from themselves:

> [...] philosophizing is, first and foremost, self-taught [...] likewise, 'self-taught' doesn't mean that you don't learn anything from others. It just means that you can't learn anything from them if they don't teach you how to unlearn. The philosophical course is not propagated as knowledge that is transmitted by acquisition (LYOTARD, 1993, p. 120-121).

Enabling students to develop independent and critical thinking, i.e. to experiment with thinking individually, is the main task of philosophy. This training is important for the development of the human being and the citizen, as it encourages them to seek out new experiences and new ways of thinking about the world.

Secondary school is generally considered to be a phase of structure and discovery for adolescents, who are in the process of formation. In this way, Renata Aspis and Silvio Gallo (2009, p. 116) show us that: "[...] philosophical thinking is rethinking, ruminating, [...] creating philosophical concepts and meta-creation". In this process, we also need to evaluate in order to know where we are going in this organization of such a complex dimension that is philosophizing.

Transformation through Philosophy becomes a reference point for the individual who is in the process of formation, instigating them to consider the meaning of existence and the world, facilitating the discovery of their role in society. The broadening of knowledge through this subject is essential if students are not to perceive themselves as fractional beings, as they will have a vision of the whole. In this way, students can see themselves as members of a whole, of a society, which can help them consolidate their moral, ethical and political development, etc.

We therefore need to rethink the process of teaching/learning philosophy, as well as its role in secondary and undergraduate education, so that this teaching can be representative and meaningful for the subjects involved.

REFERENCES

ASPIS, Renata; GALLO, Silvio. **Teaching Philosophy**: a book for teachers. Atta Midia e Educapao: Sao Paulo, 2009.

BRASIL. **Law No. 9364** (LDBEN), of December 16, 1996. Available at: <http://www.jusbrasil.com.br/legislacao>. Accessed on July 12, 2011.

CAVALCANTE, Jhoanya da Silva. **Teaching Philosophy in High School:** Challenges and Perspectives. Monograph presented to the Philosophy course at the State University of Roraima - UERR. Supervisor: Elemar Kleber Favreto. 2011.

CHAUI, Marilena. *What is being an educator today? From art to citizenship:* the death of the educator. In: BRANDAO, C. *et all.* **The educator today.** 10.ed. Rio de Janeiro: Graal, 1992, p. 51-70.

COSTA, Joao Cruz. *The situation of philosophical teaching in Brazil.* In: **Panorama da Historia da Filosofia no Brasil**. Sao Paulo: Cultrix, 1959.

DELEUZE, Gilles. GUATTARI, Felix. **What is Philosophy?** 2.ed. Translated by Bento Prado Jr. and Alberto Alonso Munoz. Rio de Janeiro: 34, 1997.

GALLO, Silvio; KOHAN, Walter. *Criticism of some commonplaces when thinking about Philosophy in Secondary Education.* In: KOHAN, Walter O. (org.) **Filosofia no Ensino Medio**. Rio de Janeiro: Vozes, 2000, Vol. VI.

GELAMO, Rodrigo Pelloso. *The Problem of Experience in Philosophy Teaching.* **Educapao e Realidade**, vol. 31, n°. 2, Marilia: UNESP, 2006, p. 09-26.

GONQALVES, Julio Cesar; SILVA, Divino Jose da. *Philosopher versus philosophy teacher* - The teaching of philosophy and the training of philosopher teachers. **Saber Academico**, n ° 11,2011. ISSN 1980-5950, p. 70-85.

FAVARETTO, Celso. *On the teaching of philosophy.* **Revista da Faculdade de Educapao**, USP, 19, 1993, p. 97 - 102.

LYOTARD, Jean-Frangois. **The postmodern.** Translated by Ricardo Correia Barbosa. *4th* ed. Rio de Janeiro: Jose Olympio, 1993.

MAGUE, Jean. *The teaching of Philosophy:* its guidelines. **Revista Brasileira de Estudos Pedagogicos**. Rio de Janeiro, V.5, fasc. 4, n. 20, 1955, p. 642-649. (Documentario Filosofia no Brasil).

MENEZES, Luis Carlos de. *Training teachers:* the university's task. In: CATANI, Denice; MIRANDA, Hercilia; MENEZES, Luis Carlos; FISCHMANN, Roseli (Orgs.). **University, School and Teacher Training**. Sao Paulo: Brasiliense, 1986.

MORAES, Amaury. *A importância da didatica para (a formacao de) o professor de Filosofia*. Sao Paulo: FEUSP, 2001.

NOVOA, Antonio. *School-Society Relations:* new answers to an old problem. In: SERBINO, Raquel V.; RIBEIRO, Ricardo; BARBOSA, Raquel; GEBRAN, Raimunda (Orgs.). **Teacher Training**. Sao Paulo: Fundagao Editora da UNESP, 1998, p. 19-39. (Seminars and Debates)

SILVA, Franklin Leopoldo e. *Historia da Filosofia:* Centro ou Referenda? In: NIELSEN NETO, H. (org.) **O Ensino de Filosofia no 2. Grau**. Sao Paulo: SEAF/SOFIA, 1986.

TOMAZETTI, Elisete M. *Filosofia no ensino medio e seu professor,* algumas reflexoes. **Educagao, vol. 27, n° 02,** Santa Maria: UFSM, 2002, p. 21-30. Available at: <http://coralx.ufsm.br/revce/revce/2002/02/a7.htm>. Accessed on: November 20, 2012.

CHAPTER III

THE APPLICABILITY OF GILLES DELEUZE AND FELIX GUATTARI'S PEDAGOGY OF CONCEPT AND CREATIVE PHILOSOPHY IN THE TEACHING OF PHILOSOPHY

Marcos Silveira Aranguiz Claudio Sipert

INITIAL CONSIDERATIONS

We begin with the following phrase: "every concept has a history", pointed out by the authors of the text *"What is philosophy?"*, Gilles Deleuze and Felix Guattari. For them, this statement is obvious, because the multiplicity that forms concepts comes from other concepts, which are related to problems (or can be) and to planes of immanence. In this becoming, generated by (de)territorialization and in the infinity of possibilities that we see in the structure of the concept, we can trace a "history" of this complex process, after all, nothing comes from nothing (*ex nihilo, nihil fit*[2]), and the concept arises from something and comes to possess a history in its constant becoming. So, what are the components of a philosophy and how can we articulate them?

Firstly, the multiplicity in the history and nature of the concept in its present becoming and connections (bridges) results in the idea of multiple and created components. Secondly, concepts are distinct, heterogeneous and have endo-consistency in unity, after all, they have irregular contours, and their boundaries define inner consistency. Thirdly, the concept itself is considered to be the meeting point of the components, because the conceptual point, as an intensive stroke, runs through and is present in all the components of the concept. The concept is a heterogenesis, "[...] an ordering of its components by neighborhood zones" (DELEUZE; GUATTARI, 1992, p. 9). These three conceptual components, added to the plane of immanence and the conceptual characters, form the structure of philosophy as conceptual creation in the understanding of the *event.* But what is the event? What are its characteristics?

The concept-event is embodied. It only exists because it insists on something in the world (a kind of materialism), but, as a pure singularity, different, it is embodied in bodies, but it is different from the things it relates to and depends on. "The concept

---

[2] Famous and commonly requested in the medieval period.

says the event, not the essence or the thing itself, so it is incorporeal" (FAVRETO, 2013, p. 21).

For Deleuze and Guattari (1992), thinking is looking at the event, trying to understand it (the task of philosophy), and asking what it is. Therefore, unlike Heidegger for example (for whom only philosophy "thinks"), the two authors of the text propose other forms of encounter with thought, because, from this perspective, thinking about the event is not exclusive to philosophy. Philosophy questions the thing by creating concepts of its own; this would be the first form of encounter. Science, on the other hand, describes things and draws perspectives through a process of cause and effect. Finally, the authors point to art as another encounter with thought, which is geared towards a sensitive involvement with the thing, producing percepts and affects. These three forms are related to the event, but each in its own way.

The event, therefore, is the plane from which the concept emerges, and both are singular. Unlike entities, which necessarily have an identity, concept-events are pure singularities, and, in this sense, pure difference, multiplicity. Knowledge and difference, and concept and knowledge, concepts are multiple because they have a history in their becoming, because they have other concepts in and around their own structure. By nature, concepts are multiple, heterogeneous, a self-referential surface.

After this brief exposition of the concept for Deleuze and Guattari, we will try to demonstrate, in the course of this chapter, the relationship established between the concept of philosophy, already presented, and its basic onto-epistemological structure, as well as with the teaching of Philosophy itself, in order to clarify its possibility of application in an educational system.

THE DOGMATIC IMAGE OF THOUGHT AND ITS THREE BASIC OPERATIONS

According to the thinking of Gilles Deleuze (and, to a certain extent, Felix Guattari), philosophical translation would be dogmatic, attached to a moral image of thought, as Nietzsche had already postulated. This dogmatism, pointed out as a "dogmatic image of thought", is mainly responsible for Plato, because thinking through these images is thinking in a transcendent model, in the same way that we see in his philosophy, in other words, thinking through the (imperfect) representation of a form, model, idea (FAVRETO, 2013).

Given this framework, the three basic operations present in the Dogmatic

Image of Thought are: contemplation, reflection and communication. Contemplation requires an object, creating a representation. This object must be given and obviously exist, or pre-exist. An image is extracted from this object and, for this reason, for Deleuze, in contemplation there is no difference, just as there is no immanence, we simply produce a transcendent image without any impulse of "productive creation". The second basic operation is reflection, which is not exclusive to the philosopher. The philosopher's differential in relation to reflection is the removal of *"doxa",* opinion, which hinders the philosophical act itself and proves to be an enemy of philosophy - "reflection, as the organization of an opinion, is the postulation of a unity" (FAVRETO, 2013, p. 17). Finally, we have communication, which is related to consensus. Through this operation we have the demarcation that separates the "rational" from the "non-rational". By overcoming chaos, rationality becomes a kind of absolute opinion, while what is considered non-rational must be condemned and confined.

DECONSTRUCTION AND THE NEW IMAGE OF THOUGHT

In the works studied, we see Deleuzian deconstruction through a new type of approach: "The New Image of Thought". The deconstruction itself moves philosophy away from the egide of the four roots of representation pointed out by Foucault, breaking the dogmatic axis to leave only the image of thought, which becomes a plate in this attempt to reverse Platonism, formed by a plane of immanence, conceptual characters and, above all, the creation of concepts.

It begins with the tracing of a plane of immanence, which, in a way, is still in a pre-philosophical ambit, since the "image of thought" can be without presuppositions or full of preconceptions (field of transcendence). So Deleuzo-Guattarian philosophy, like contemporary philosophy in general, aims for a new image of thought, which, for these thinkers, should not be tied to models and needs this plane (plane of immanence) for concepts to emerge. This first step stands in contrast to simple contemplation: what exists is only the plane of immanence, and it is there that the philosopher creates his concepts, without having to resort to a transcendent plane. This creation of concepts doesn't come out of nowhere, but rather as a kind of "migration" of concepts from other philosophers or planes of immanence. However, as the creator of a plane of immanence, this philosopher doesn't reproduce the concept extracted from the philosophy of another, but by placing it on his plane, the concept gains a new meaning valid for that plane, in the process already mentioned above, known as deterritorialization and reterritorialization of the concept. This is how the Deleuzo-Guattarian creation of concepts takes place. And this creation will allow the philosopher to create a *new image of thought,* which is an image not linked to the model[3] , because without a model there are no presuppositions or "pre-concepts". According to Favreto (2013, p. 19):

> The thinker is only formed and only builds his philosophy when he brings a plane of immanence. But we can't think of the plane of immanence separately from the other two philosophical operations pointed out by Deleuze and Guattari [...], the invention of characters and the creation of concepts. [...] Philosophy only sprouts when these three operations are put to work together.

This implies that in order to create concepts, the philosopher must create a plane of immanence. The event is the concept itself, and both are incorporeal, with the concept being the enunciation of the event. In order for this interaction between the bodies to take place, culminating in the event/concept, the presence of a conceptual character is indispensable, which is the voice of the philosopher himself, and can take any form, or even be the philosopher himself. It is this character who, within the plane of immanence, will interact with bodies to generate concepts/events. This is how Deleuzo-Guattarian philosophy detaches itself from the transcendent plane, because it creates its concepts from the interaction between the bodies present on the plane of immanence, which can be interpreted as life itself, life as pure immanence. This means that "[...] we must understand that life itself is full of events and encounters between bodies" (FAVRETO, 2013, p. 23).

Once the plane of immanence has been swallowed up, the conceptual character must emerge, who, according to FAVRETO (2013, p. 19), is "[...] a legitimate creator of concepts and also the one who articulates this whole mesh of concepts created and acted upon in a given philosophy". Therefore, he is not simply a character who narrates the story; the philosopher himself serves his characters, who interact with the concepts of the created plane of immanence.

Philosophy is based on the plane of immanence, conceptual characters and

---

[3] It is understood that it is not linked to the model because as long as philosophers are attached to a transcendental model, all the concepts created based on that model will always be copies of it. As soon as the philosopher detaches himself from the Transcendental Ideal, the concepts present in the philosophies are no longer linked to the Forms. To use an example, Nietzsche's concepts, present in the Deleuzian work, are not recreated, but created in a different meaning, because they are inserted, from then on, in the Deleuzian plane of immanence.

the creation of concepts. The problems arise on the plane of immanence, and the conceptual characters delimit the plane itself from the concepts. Every concept is multiple (even those based on others), it can be represented by any sign, in other words, it is itself that which lies behind the sign (by showing the sign, we have the totality of the concept). The concept, from this perspective, is the ultimate end, the event itself (concept-event), occurring when the plate is folded, which can only be perceived through this folding, and this folding occurs with the action of the conceptual character. These three basic operations are the counterpoint presented by Deleuze and Guattari to the three instances of the dogmatic image of thought, generating, according to Favreto (2013), three philosophical readings related to philosophy teaching: 1) discursive multiplicity on education, 2) combating the three classical functions of philosophy and 3) life understood as pure immanence.

FINAL CONSIDERATIONS

Philosophy, from the point of view addressed here, can be called a "Creative Philosophy", because its proposal goes against the grain of the entire classical philosophical tradition, which proposes a deepening of the images of thought that have already been conceived. For Deleuze and Guattari, the philosophical tradition has always been guided by a "Dogmatic Image of Thought", which begins with Plato, identifying the Perfect Ideas, the *eidos of* things, with the entire philosophical tradition endorsing this search for the Model (which ends up becoming a dogma); whether in Aristotle or Kant, philosophy has always been a recreation of the same. The same search for "Truth", "Beauty" and "Goodness", only changing the direction to reach the Universal.

Favreto (2013), based on Deleuze and Guattari, suggests the "Pedagogy of the Concept", based on the "New Image of Thought", which would be precisely the creation of concepts in an immanent way, and not by repeating the process of searching for the *transcendent eidos.* Based on the Philosophy of Difference (initiated by Nietzsche), Deleuze and Guattari deconstruct Platonism, which persisted during philosophical translation, criticizing the basis of dogmatic philosophical thought (based on contemplation, reflection and communication, where all things are linked in a transcendent, unified and representative way), proposing a new way of doing philosophy. This way corresponds to swallowing a plane of immanence, inventing conceptual characters and creating concepts. This philosophy has the status of *creator* because every time we talk about a concept that has already been developed on another plane, we are not talking about concept X of philosopher Y, but rather bringing the concept to its own plane of immanence and transforming its meaning. For this reason, philosophy would always be a creator, not a reproducer of concepts.

The proposal of the French authors, "[...] in constructing their philosophy, [is] a philosophy that aims to be free of presuppositions and prejudices, since they [the presuppositions] cause a given thought to be transformed into dogmatic knowledge" (FAVRETO, 2013, p. 15). And the concept of "pedagogy of the concept" is an attempt to show the way to a creative philosophy, which would be detached from dogmatism, since it would not be bound by models *(eidos,* Universals), but rather, as Favreto (2013, p. 17) points out, philosophy "[...] throws itself into the purest multiplicity, it jumps into the chaotic abyss to return to the surface and create its concepts". The process of a creative philosophy is precisely to break the idea, so perpetuated, that doing philosophy is reproducing images. This process goes hand in hand with Difference, because it is crucial to thinking about philosophy without the Transcendent plane.

And what would be the relationship between this Deleuzo-Guattarian proposal and education? At this point, we look to Renata Aspis and Silvio Gallo, who lead the research that follows the path presented so far (and in a way always verify and corroborate the applicability of the concept of creative philosophy to education) for a proposal that questions the current model of philosophy teaching, which only presents the history of philosophy as absolute (dogmatic), which must be learned in the same way as it was left by the philosophers, so that the educator makes his students mere reproducers of ideas, as Favreto (2013, p. 15) states, showing how creative philosophy can be applied to education. 15), showing how creative philosophy would have a much broader and more beneficial role for students. In this case, the educator himself would be a philosopher. Therefore, the philosopher-educator would show his students the history of philosophy as a "sea of chaos", from which they should emerge and, by observing the chaos, create their own concepts. Thus transforming education from reproductive and mechanistic to creative and holistic.

For Favreto (2013, p. 22), there are therefore three ways of approaching this issue: "the multiplicity of discourse on education, the fight against the three classical functions of philosophy and life understood as pure immanence".

The multiplicity of discourse on education would concern the philosopher as educator, who, as I said, still operates in the shadow of classical philosophy, but who should think that education can be approached in different ways, whether scientifically, artistically, politically or methodologically. They should stop reproducing discourses that are often not even proper to philosophy. This philosopher-educator should turn to thinking about education philosophically, striving to bring about a plane of immanence and establish a philosophy.

The fight against the three classical functions of philosophy would take place when philosophy, seen as a creator of concepts, sets out to deconstruct the three basic pillars of the classical philosophical tradition, which are contemplation, reflection and communication. These three operations characterize the perpetuation of an already established system, which is the reproduction of Forms (Models, *Aeids,* Universals), which French philosophers have already pointed out the error of continuing to reproduce copies of Transcendent Forms, without actually creating new concepts, based on a plane of immanence.

Life understood as pure immanence leads them to understand life as the very plane of immanence where events "insist", since what exists are bodies, the event is pure insistence, and this insistence is also a concept, which is formed in the interaction of everything and everyone (the bodies). Pure immanence, present in life, mixes the two times named by Deleuze as *Aion* and *Chronos,* which are, respectively, the unlimited (past and future at the same time) and the limited (the present, where there is corporeality and existence). It is on this plane of immanence, life as pure immanence, that philosophers show the possibility of creating concepts, because as long as time is present, everything is, everything can be said about bodies, but when it becomes the past, or even a future project, it is inconstant. An inconstancy that doesn't symbolize the fragility of not knowing what it is, but rather that it is always changing due to the constant interaction between bodies:

> These events are incorporeal and pass through us, changing us profoundly with each new event. In this sense, the self is no longer the self, since this event has changed it in such a way that the self that presents itself in this state of affairs is no longer the same as the one that presented itself in the previous state (FAVRETO, 2013, p. 23).

In this way, the philosopher-educator is the one who creates his own plane of immanence from life itself, and with it he begins to transmit to his students not more copies of models, but the possibility of creating concepts, perceived in the very immanence of life, which can allow them to modify it, since events end up constantly transforming the relationship between bodies.

The concept of creative philosophy could therefore be a good alternative for thinking about the teaching of philosophy, given that much is taught about the history of philosophy and little is taught about philosophizing. Perhaps this flaw should be corrected in the training of these teachers, who leave the academy with the ideal that philosophy can only be done by great philosophers, and that any other type of thought is inferior to it. What Deleuze and Guattari show us is that both science (prospects) and art (affects) think, but what differentiates them from philosophy is that it is the only one capable of thinking in concepts.

Starting from ontology and epistemology, briefly mentioned in this chapter, we have the basis of the history of philosophy as a starting point for the student and for conceptual creation itself as its point of arrival, a process that takes place through the creation of "subversions" of the major versions, seen as dogmatic images of thought. From this perspective, the teacher's role becomes to create possibilities that allow this production of subversions of the history of philosophy, of the world, of reality and of society; as if it were a form of ordering the subjective and individual chaos embodied in this sub-version, which, even though it is minor, could never be considered less important.

REFERENCES

ASPIS, Renata Lima; GALLO, Silvio. **Teaching philosophy**: a book for teachers.

Sao Paulo: Atta media and Education, 2009.

DELEUZE, Gilles. **Difference and repetition.** Trad. Luiz Orlandi, Roberto Machado. 2. ed. Rio de Janeiro: Graal, 2006.

and GUATTARI, Felix. **What is philosophy?** Trad. Bento Prado Jr. and Alberto Alonso Munoz. Rio de Janeiro: Ed. 34, 1992 (TRANS Collection).

FAVRETO, Elemar Kleber. The philosopher educator and creative philosophy - An analysis of Deleuze and Guattari's 'pedagogy of the concept'. **Polymatheia** (Online), v. 06, p. 14-25, 2013.

ZOURABICHVILI, Frangois. **Deleuze's vocabulary.** Translated by Andre Telles. Andre Telles. Rio de Janeiro: Relume Dumara, 2004 (Conexoes; 24).

CHAPTER IV

NOTES ON THE TEACHING OF PHILOSOPHY AND THE SOCIO-EDUCATIONAL REALITY IN HIGH SCHOOLS IN THE MUNICIPALITY OF CAROEBE/RR

Cleudicelia Lopes Xavier Waldemar Moura Vilhena Junior

INITIAL CONSIDERATIONS

The teaching of philosophy in Brazilian basic education, despite having its history marked by various interruptions and facing difficulties in its implementation, has great relevance in the formation of our young people, since we live in a society highly marked by constant contradictions. This requires teaching based on reflection and daily analysis of reality. In this sense, we understand that teaching philosophy is necessary, since high school students need to be encouraged to reflect and seek to understand the complexity of the world around them. According to Aspis (2004, p. 310), philosophy lessons should be a place for philosophical experiences. In this line of reasoning, philosophy lessons need to aim to "[...] offer philosophical criteria for the student to judge reality through the practice of philosophical questioning and the construction of concepts, through the exercise of philosophical creativity and evaluation". This way of teaching philosophy is capable of giving young people a new outlook on reality, a self-conscious or metacognitive outlook.

With this in mind, the question arose of how the teaching and learning of philosophy is practiced in the municipality of Caroebe/RR. To this end, the aim was to understand the reality surrounding the teaching of high school philosophy in schools in the municipality of Caroebe/RR. The specific objectives were: to analyze the historical context of the teaching of Philosophy in Brazil; to point out the legal frameworks that govern the teaching of Philosophy in Brazil; to analyze how the teaching of Philosophy is practiced in the schools of Caroebe. As a methodology, we adopted field research with a qualitative approach, using a questionnaire with open questions as a data collection tool in order to collect data on the philosophy teachers at the three state high schools in the municipality. The data was analyzed from a qualitative perspective.

The text is organized into six topics: Brief Historical Context of Philosophy Teaching in Brazil; Legal Aspects of Philosophy Teaching in Basic Education;

Philosophy Teaching in High Schools in the Municipality of Caroebe/RR; What Does the Research Reveal? Results and Discussions; Teacher Training by Knowledge Area; and Final Considerations. We hope that this work will contribute to understanding the scenario surrounding the teaching of Philosophy in the municipality of Caroebe and that it will also serve as a reflection on the problems observed in Basic Education as a whole, in order to overcome them.

BRIEF HISTORICAL CONTEXT OF PHILOSOPHY TEACHING IN BRAZIL

When we analyze the historical context of philosophy teaching in Brazil, we can see that it has been marked by incessant comings and goings in the basic education curriculum. At times it has been made compulsory, at others it has been considered a supplementary subject and at times it has even been abolished. According to Gallo (2012), several authors have dedicated themselves to studying the history of philosophy teaching in Brazil, but Alves (2002) points out that:

> He classifies the presence of philosophy in Brazilian high school curricula as follows: guaranteed presence, in the colonial period up to the Republic; undefined presence, from the first republic to the civil-military coup of 1964; defined absence, in the dictatorial period after 1964; and, finally, controlled presence, in the period of political "redemocratization" after 1980 (ALVES, 2002 *apud* GALLO, 2012, p. 51).

The historical analysis of philosophy teaching also reveals the contradictions that marked its introduction into Brazilian education. In the colonial period, when it was introduced in Brazil, it was done mainly to please two interests. Firstly, the interests of the Catholic Church, since the Jesuits were the philosophy teachers, and secondly, to serve the interests of the colonial elite. According to Lagos Rodrigues (2012, p. 70), "[...] in colonial Brazil, the teaching of philosophy was offered in a small number of colleges, where scholasticism was the basis of teaching, due to the religious ties of the Jesuits, who were responsible for education at the time". This fact proves our assertion that philosophy served the interests of the Catholic Church. As for serving the interests of the colonial elite, Oliveira and Oliveira (2012) state that as early as the 16th century, philosophy teaching served political interests, since it was aimed at the ruling class who educated the children of landlords.

In this sense, they also point out that:

Philosophy, as a teaching practice in Brazil, emerged in this context of colonization with the arrival of the Jesuits. The religious character given to education at the time was established as the proper model for the teaching of philosophy, whose purpose was the bookish and rhetorical erudition of the ruling classes, the repetition and memorization of philosophical systems, the formation of literate, erudite and Catholic men (OLIVEIRA; OLIVEIRA 2012, p. 3).

According to Oliveira and Oliveira (2012), Jesuit education was the basis of the Brazilian educational system in the period between the 16th and 17th centuries, until the Order was expelled in 1759 with the arrival of the Marquis of Pombal. This expulsion was due to the clash of interests between the Portuguese Crown, which had adopted the ideas of the Enlightenment, and the Religious Order, which sought to preserve its system of education, i.e. scholasticism.

Along the same lines, Lago Rodrigues (2012, p. 70) states that "[...] the conception of Philosophy disseminated in Brazilian school education has historically been linked to abstract and rationalist knowledge, linked to the education of elites". This is because, in the author's view, the scholastic foundations of philosophy teaching, since colonial Brazil, have disconnected it from the contextualized characteristics of teaching geared to the reality of life, causing, in a way, the removal of possibilities for reflection and problematization.

This leads us to realize that from the very beginning of the introduction of philosophy teaching in Brazil, the contradiction has accompanied it closely. This contradiction is understood when Lago Rodrigues (2012) points out that until the middle of the 20th century, teaching and philosophical knowledge in Brazil were characterized by idealistic, rational and pragmatic views.

LEGAL ASPECTS OF TEACHING PHILOSOPHY IN BASIC EDUCATION

In the history of the legal aspects of the teaching of Philosophy in Brazil, we can see that since the promulgation of the country's first Law of Guidelines and Bases of Education, Law 4.024/61, the teaching of Philosophy, which was a compulsory subject in religious schools, was aimed at the country's social and economic elites[4] , becoming part of the list of complementary subjects, which may or may not be chosen

---

[4] According to Lago Rodrigues (2012, p. 71), "[...] with the Capanema Reform, in 1942, the teaching of Philosophy became compulsory, especially in religious schools, which catered for the country's social and economic elites".

by schools to complement their curriculum alongside compulsory subjects (GALLO, 2012).

The situation, which was already bad, worsened after the military coup of 1964, when the subject was removed from the school curriculum and replaced by Moral and Civil Education. This completely changed the direction of teaching. While Philosophy teaching sought to develop "critical and transformative thinking", Moral and Civil Education went in the opposite direction, i.e. its main objective was catechist and ideological activity at a political level. In fact, the aim was to prepare people to obey the prevailing order, defending the *status quo* (CARTOLANO, 1985 *apud* FAVERO, 2004).

In this sense, Lago Rodrigues (2012, p. 71) points out that:

> Law 5.692, enacted in 1971, in the midst of the military regime, abolished Philosophy from the curriculum, which led to the reactions and mobilizations that took place in the country in favour of its maintenance/return to the school curriculum. These mobilizations stimulated reactions at various levels and, by means of Opinion 7.044/82 of the then Federal Education Council (CFE), possibilities were opened up for the return of the Philosophy subject to secondary school curricula.

According to Gallo (2012), the end of the military dictatorship, which began the process of re-democratization in Brazil, marked the struggle of those who, since the 1980s, had been demanding the return of philosophy in the education of young Brazilians, so that these demands were, to a certain extent, met through the enactment of the new Law of Guidelines and Bases of Education, Law No. 9.394/96. Partially because after a long process of discussion with organized civil society, which had envisioned philosophy returning to the curriculum as a compulsory subject in Basic Education, the movements realized that the new law had been changed and that the approval text presented philosophy no longer as a compulsory subject, but as "content necessary for the exercise of citizenship".

The dissatisfaction of those in favor of making philosophy a compulsory subject in basic education was only put to an end in June 2008, with the entry into force of Law No. 11.684, which made the teaching of philosophy and sociology compulsory in the three grades of secondary education. As a result, the two subjects were once again incorporated into the secondary school curriculum. However, we know that currently the teaching of philosophy in Brazilian secondary schools is once again going through moments of instability and insecurity. Just remember that there has recently been a new reform of secondary education, proposing new changes to its curriculum.

Among several issues raised, one of them is that the changes did not take into account many of the discussions and decisions already made by the National Education Plan, which, since 2014, had been trying to build a path for improving Brazilian education. Against the backdrop of these dialogues, and as a matter of urgency, a new law was quickly passed, causing changes to the main law governing Brazilian education, as can be seen in the initial text of Law No. 13.415/17:

> Amends Laws No. 9.394, of December 20, 1996, which establishes the guidelines and bases of national education, and No. 11.494, of June 20, 2007, which regulates the Fund for the Maintenance and Development of Basic Education and the Valorization of Education Professionals, the Consolidation of Labor Laws CLT, approved by Decree Law No. 5.452, of May 1, 1943, and Decree Law No. 236, of February 28, 1967; repeals Law No. 11.161, of August 5, 2005; and establishes the Policy for Promoting the Implementation of Full-Time High Schools (BRASIL, 2017, p. 1).

It is not our intention to analyze in depth the various changes proposed by Law No. 13.415/17, but we would like to point out the concerns it raises in relation to the teaching of Philosophy, the subject of our research. By analyzing the text of the law, we can see that the only subjects considered compulsory in the three grades of secondary school will be mathematics, Portuguese and English. In relation to philosophy, the law states in Art. 35-A, "§ 2° The National Common Curricular Base for Secondary Education will compulsorily include studies and practices in physical education, art, sociology and philosophy". Furthermore, Art.
36, of Law No. 13.415/17, states that:

> The secondary education curriculum will be made up of the National Common Curriculum Base and training itineraries, which should be organized by offering different curricular arrangements, according to the relevance to the local context and the possibilities of the education systems, namely:
> I - languages and their technologies;
> II - mathematics and its technologies;
> III - natural sciences and their technologies;
> IV - humanities and applied social sciences;
> V   - technical and professional training.

However, what is most intriguing about this scenario of changes is that at the same time as the government seems to want to urgently resolve the problems that actually involve Brazilian secondary education, it is also clear that the National Common Curriculum Base for Secondary Education, which is given the task by Law No. 13.415/17 of explaining how the new Secondary Education will be organized, or rather, what and how the content and subjects will be taught.

On December 20, 2017, the President of the Republic approved the final text of the Common National Curriculum Base for Early Childhood Education and Primary Education. However, the BNCC for Secondary Education is still being voted on by the National Education Council (CNE). We won't go into the issues surrounding this subject.

Having learned a little more about the history of philosophy teaching in Brazil, we set out to analyze the reality in which we find ourselves. In this way, we present below our perception of the scenario involving secondary schools in the municipality of Caroebe/RR.

THE TEACHING OF PHILOSOPHY IN HIGH SCHOOLS IN THE MUNICIPALITY OF CAROEBE/RR

The municipality of Caroebe is one of the fifteen municipalities in the state of Roraima, created by Law No. 082, of November 4, 1994, with lands dismembered from the municipality of Sao Joao da Baliza. It was established in 1997. The municipality is located in the micro-region of Southeast Roraima, meso-region of Southern Roraima, 338 km from Boa Vista. According to IBGE data[5] (2017), Caroebe's population is currently estimated at 9,473 inhabitants. In the 2010 census, it had 8,114 people, resulting in a population density of 0.67 inhabitants/km^2 . Below is a map of the municipality of Caroebe.

---

[5] Data available at: https://cidades.ibge.gov.br/brasil/rr/caroebe/panorama.

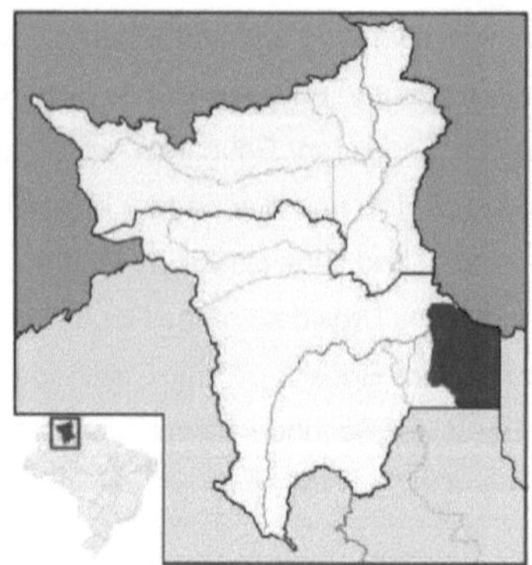

Figure 1: Location of the municipality of Caroebe on the map of the state of
Roraima
Source: Wikipedia, 2018.

In an attempt to understand the scenario surrounding the teaching of
Philosophy in the municipality of Caroebe, we came up with the following questions to
guide our research. How many secondary schools are there in Caroebe? How is
philosophy taught? What training do the teachers who teach philosophy have in
Caroebe? In order to answer these questions, we used field research, in which we
collected data by visiting schools and administering questionnaires to philosophy
teachers. In this questionnaire, we asked the following questions: Age; Sex; What is
your background?; How long have you been working with philosophy?; What teaching
materials do you use in your classes?; Does the school make teaching materials
available to students? Which ones? Have you taught other subjects?; What subjects
do you currently work with? How many classes are you currently working with
(year/grade and subjects)?

Our objective with the questionnaire was to verify the context surrounding the
teaching of Philosophy practiced by teachers in Caroebe, showing a little about the
reality of each teacher and how they developed their work in the classroom.

WHAT DOES THE RESEARCH REVEAL? RESULTS AND DISCUSSIONS

During the research, we found that the municipality of Caroebe has three high
schools[6] . They are Escola Estadual Tereza Teodoro de Oliveira, located at BR 210,

---

[6] It is worth noting that the survey does not include the indigenous area of the municipality, which also

km 96 S/N - Centro; Escola Estadual Clovis Nova da Costa, located at BR210, km 118 - Zona Rural; and Escola Estadual Professor Vidal da Penha Ferreira, located at Rua Marco Antonio Vieira Costa s/n vila, Entre Rios, district of Caroebe.

In the three schools surveyed, we found that the teaching of philosophy is summarized in Marilena Chaui's "Invitation to Philosophy", since this is the only bibliography used by the teachers. According to Teixeira, Almeida and Silva (2012, p.09), when analyzing Chaui's work, they argue that " [...] although the content is distributed around concepts or a disciplinary approach to philosophy, the agenda is tied to the historical bias. In other words, the teachability of philosophy obeys the principle of the history of philosophy". Favero *et al* (2004, p. 274) state that:

> Even good quality texts, such as Marilena de Souza Chaui's, perhaps the most prestigious of any in the country, are considered too 'heavy' by teachers (440 pages long and in a very 'academic' style) and presuppose an excessively classical conception of philosophy and its teaching.

A teaching system where only one bibliographic reference is used already hinders both student interest and learning in relation to the subject, in addition to the fact that there aren't enough books in schools for students to have more contact with philosophy content. Of the three schools surveyed, only the Teresa Teodoro de Oliveira State School has books for students. However, they are kept in the school library since it is not enough for all the students.

As a result, most students' contact with books is restricted to just one philosophy lesson a week. It's worth noting that the students who live in rural areas are the most affected by this situation, since when the teacher does some research work, they don't even have access to the books that are in the school library, miles away from their homes, nor do they have access to the internet, and they end up developing texts with empty concepts and without any reflection. In this sense, the teaching of philosophy in Caroebe follows the traditional mold of the famous "I pretend to teach, you pretend to learn", since the students are solely at the mercy of the teacher's explanations in the classroom.

Brazilian philosopher Renata Aspis (2004) argues that philosophy teaching should aim to be a philosophical experience. According to the author:

> Philosophizing is a discipline of thought which, as it operates, produces

---

has secondary schools.

According to the author, "[...] the teaching of philosophy to young people in school is justified if it is the teaching of the creation of concepts that deal with their problems" (ASPIS, 2004, p. 305). Unfortunately, this is not what we found in Caroebe's schools. The explanation for teaching with strong encyclopedic characteristics in the schools surveyed is perhaps due to the fact that in all of them we didn't find any teachers with a degree in philosophy, nor did they receive any training to work with this subject. Of the three teachers interviewed, only one has a background in philosophy.

The teacher at Escola Estadual Teresa Teodoro de Oliveira has a bachelor's degree in Theology and an initial degree in Pedagogy. He said in the questionnaire that he had been working with philosophy at the school for six years. When asked if he had ever worked with other subjects, he said he had worked with history, geography and mathematics. He currently works with philosophy, sociology and religious education. In all, he teaches 26 classes, including students from the 9th grade of elementary school to the 3rd grade of high school.

At Clovis Nova da Costa State School, we found that the subject of philosophy is the responsibility of the school's Portuguese language teacher. She has a degree in Pedagogy and a second degree in Letters, and works with Portuguese language, philosophy, sociology and arts. In all, she teaches four classes, which include students from the 9th grade of elementary school to the 3rd grade of high school. When we asked her how long she had been working with philosophy, she revealed that, until December 2017, she had only been working there for five months, when she was hired by the state government and assigned to the school in question. Before that, according to data provided by the school, the subject was not taught at the school in 2017.

The high school students at Clovis Nova da Costa State School had only five months of philosophy lessons in 2017. That's not counting the classes that couldn't be taught. As this school is located in a rural area and caters specifically for students from the countryside, it is completely dependent on school transport, which is often lacking. Sometimes due to lack of fuel, sometimes due to late payment of the drivers, sometimes due to mechanical problems. As a result, whenever the bus has any of these problems, lessons at the school are suspended, as most of the students have no other way of getting to school than by school transport.

In the last school surveyed, the Professor Vidal da Penha Ferreira State School, we found another teacher with a degree in Pedagogy and Literature, teaching philosophy. When asked about her experience with philosophy, this teacher said that she had been teaching the subject for over ten years. She also pointed out in the questionnaire that there is no teacher with a degree in philosophy in the locality and that in 2017 she was assigned to the subject to complete her 40-hour week. In all, the teacher works in Portuguese and philosophy with students from the 6th year of elementary school to the 3rd year of secondary school, in a total of eight classes. When asked if she had ever taught other subjects, she replied: "I haven't worked with chemistry, physics or Spanish".

In view of the data collected, what most caught our attention was the realization that the teaching of philosophy in Caroebe is entirely the responsibility of people who have no training in the area, mainly Pedagogy graduates, who, after the state's framework law, Law No. 892, of January 25, 2013, which provides for the creation of the Plan of Positions, Careers and Remunerations for Basic Education Servants in the State of Roraima (PCCREB), were forced to take on subjects considered less demanding in terms of specific training.

Favero *et al* (2004, p. 256), when checking the situation of philosophy teaching in schools in Rio de Janeiro, found a similar situation to that found in Caroebe. According to the authors, "[...] the situation of the teachers is precarious, as in many parts of the country, with many of them trained in subjects other than philosophy, being transferred to teach the subject via the 'priority allocation bonus' (GLP)". Unfortunately, the situation continues to repeat itself even thirteen years after the authors' research.

Analyzing the reality of the schools in Caroebe, we note that not only is philosophy being taught by teachers without specific qualifications, but the very relevance of specific training is much criticized in the state of Roraima, given the reality of the schools and the interior of the state. In this way, such training proves to be ineffective, since in practice teachers are forced to work in other subjects, either to complete their workload or because of the small number of teachers in schools in the interior.

TEACHER TRAINING BY SUBJECT AREA

Knowing the reality surrounding the schools surveyed and bearing in mind that all the documents that guide Brazilian Basic Education point to the organization of curricular content by knowledge area, namely: the Curricular Guidelines for Primary Education (Art. 14 and Art. 15); the Curricular Guidelines for Secondary Education (Art. 8); in addition to the recently approved Common National Curriculum Base for Primary Education. In common, we can see that all these documents are organized into four areas of knowledge: Languages, Mathematics, Natural Sciences and Human Sciences. It should also be remembered that one of the novelties presented in the reform of Secondary Education is precisely the organization of the curriculum, based on five major areas of knowledge or professional activity, namely: Languages; Mathematics; Natural Sciences; Human Sciences; and Technical and Professional Training.

We therefore feel the need to present here, albeit briefly, a discussion on teacher training by subject area. This is because such training presents itself as a possible way of overcoming the problems that surround the educational context of Caroebe in relation to the lack of specific teachers for each subject. As previously mentioned, we are living in a time when the main documents governing Brazilian education, from the National Curriculum Parameters to the recently approved National Common Core Curriculum for Primary Education, are striving to offer teaching that overcomes the fragmentation historically instituted, seeking to broaden the range of knowledge of elementary school students.

The main objective of the degrees with qualifications by area of knowledge is to provide interdisciplinary training capable of meeting this need, and they are therefore in line with the intention of these documents. However, there is still a lot of resistance to them being recognized. This is because, according to Martinazzo and Cherobini (2005, p. 59):

> The analytical, empirical, inductive and positivist model of knowledge inspired by the Cartesian method and the postulates of the modern Enlightenment brought with it, as a corollary, as well as other connotations and consequences, a simplifying, disjunctive and reductive knowledge, based on the classical principle of identity and linear, objective order.

For the aforementioned authors, overcoming this model is necessary and urgent, pointing to Edgar Morim's complexity theory as a possible way forward. Since "[...] complex knowledge enables us to understand the facts and phenomena of reality, as well as making it possible to systematize and organize information" (MARTINAZZO; CHEROBINI, 2005, p. 65). Furthermore, by appropriating the cognitive principles of complex rationality, pedagogy can promote a multidimensional and poly-ocular approach and understanding of the educational phenomenon.

In Brazil, Field Education is the forerunner of training by area of knowledge. The creation of the Program to Support Undergraduate Degrees in Rural Education (Procampo) at the Ministry of Education's Secretariat for Continuing Education, Literacy, Diversity and Inclusion (SECADI/MEC), after the II National Conference on Rural Education in 2004, initiated the training of teachers with qualifications in four areas of knowledge: Arts, Literature and Languages; Human and Social Sciences; Nature and Mathematical Sciences; and Agrarian Sciences. Molina and Antunes (2014, p. 238) state that:

> The pilot experiment to implement this public policy was then carried out at four federal universities invited by the Ministry of Education to take on the challenge (Federal University of Minas Gerais; University of Brasília; Federal University of Bahia and Federal University of Sergipe), based on recommendations from social movements, because they already had teaching, research and extension practices in rural education in their history.

According to Arroyo (2012, p. 365), Procampo "[...] advocates breaking with instrumental training and affirming a training program in which the root of everything is the human being, their process of humanization, of human emancipation". The author also states that:

> Consistent with this approach, the concept of teacher training for rural, indigenous and quilombola teachers aims to overcome the fragmentation of knowledge. (...) There is also a motivation for resisting the fragmentation in which basic education and training curricula are structured, when we think about rural education and the training of its professionals: the countryside does not develop in the fragmented logic with which technical rationality cuts up cities, in which each institution and professional field is trained to deal with a section of society. In the countryside, in the productive forms in which the various peoples organize themselves, everything is extremely articulated (ARROYO, 2012, p. 366).

In this way, we can see that Field Education degrees, by offering training by knowledge area, are meeting the changes proposed in the PCNs and the BNCC, which present curricular organization by knowledge area.

At the Federal University of Roraima, the degree course in Rural Education (LEDUCARR) was created in 2010, with the main objective of "[...] providing training for teachers who are aware of the socio-educational problems related to rural areas in order to promote the transformation of teaching as the political and social emancipation of rural areas occurs" (GABRIEL; ALBUQUERQUE, 2009, p. 07). Thus, in 2015, it graduated its first class of graduates in Rural Education, with qualifications in the following areas of knowledge: Human and Social Sciences and Natural Sciences and Mathematics.

Recently, the State University of Roraima, Rorainopolis campus, launched the entrance exam for the first degree course in Human Sciences, although it had already been working for five years with a degree course in Nature Sciences and Mathematics. When we analyzed the Course Pedagogical Project (PPC) for the Degree in Human Sciences, we saw that it also aims to train teachers from an interdisciplinary/transdisciplinary perspective. According to it:

> Although the term "transdisciplinarity" is already used in the educational context, it has not been put into practice in the classroom. For this reason, it needs to be embedded in the structure of this project for the Human Sciences Degree Course, with the aim of discussing and deepening the foundations on which the PCN is based, such as systematic and complex thinking, inter- and transdisciplinarity and their practice through methodologies such as project-based pedagogy and others that problematize situations in the learner's context. This project also aims to develop competency descriptors and build a methodology that can guide teaching through transdisciplinary projects (UERR, 2017, p. 14).

In this way, we can see that the Degree in Human Sciences will contribute to the training of educators for the interior of the state, who will be better able to understand the importance of interdisciplinary teaching, since their own training will be based on this approach. In this sense, the main objective of the Human Sciences degree course is to:

> To train teaching professionals to work as elementary school - Cycle II and high school teachers, in the areas of Philosophy, Sociology, History and Geography, based on the holistic mastery of the areas grouped into "Human Sciences" and knowledge in general lines of theoretical strands guiding the particularities and intercessions between the respective areas (UERR, 2017, p. 17).

The presence of three degrees with qualifications by area of knowledge at the two public universities in Roraima points to a way of overcoming the fragmented and simplifying teaching that has historically been practiced throughout Brazil and the world. However, as has been said, there is still a great deal of resistance to accepting and recognizing this training, and we need only mention the clash faced by the teachers who graduated from LEDUCARR during the simplified selection process for temporary substitute teachers held in April 2017.

At the time, all the teachers on the course who had signed up for the selection process had their names disqualified when the preliminary results were announced. The reasons used for the disqualifications were the same for all those who applied. Item 2.1 of the exam, which dealt with the first basic requirement for applying to the selection process in question, said: "Have a full degree in the desired area, attested to by a diploma, certificate or certificate of completion, together with an academic transcript" (SEED-RR, 2017, p. 03).

When they were disqualified, the teachers filed an appeal, explaining that they had already completed the Degree in Rural Education and that this qualified them to work in each area of knowledge. Thus, those qualified in the area of Nature Sciences and Mathematics are able to work with the subjects of chemistry, physics, biology and mathematics. Those qualified in the humanities are able to work with the subjects of history, geography, sociology and Portuguese. However, during the period when the appeals were being analyzed, they were again all rejected. It was only after a meeting between a group of representatives of the Field Education degree teachers and the vice-president of the examining committee (where it was explained that everyone had already completed the course and that it qualifies teachers to work by area of knowledge, as specified in the course's own history), that the committee pointed out that it did not recognize the course, and therefore had not denied the appeal. After much wrangling, the committee decided to recognize the course by area of knowledge and asked the course representatives to draw up a list with the names of the LEDUCARR graduates enrolled in the selection process, so that their CVs could be analyzed again. After this new analysis of the scores, several teachers were classified and subsequently hired.

Martinazzo and Cherobini (2005, p. 70) recognize that there are still many obstacles to making the transdisciplinary proposal a reality. Among the main ones they highlight:

[...] the school routine, historically constructed and pointed out by many as the main obstacle; the conformism of some professionals, who don't see the possibility of change; the conservatism of others who cling to old and outdated ideas and conceptions; the fear of change and the consequences it may bring; the absence of organized social criticism against disciplinary knowledge and the fragmentation of knowledge; the difficulty of admitting that we need to deal with uncertainty, and the lack of solidarity between men and between different peoples.

We believe that the sum of all these points shows that interdisciplinary courses are still seen in a prejudiced way in the state and in Brazil as a whole, and that there is a need to raise awareness of the problems faced in basic education in the interior of Brazil's states. It is only by raising awareness and then making people aware that this type of training can minimize these problems that we can really think clearly about the role of interdisciplinarity within academia.

FINAL CONSIDERATIONS

In view of the above, we can see that after so many years of struggle to make it a reality, philosophy teaching is still undergoing changes in terms of what it offers in Brazilian basic education. Only after the approval of the National Common Core Curriculum for Secondary Education will we have more clarity about its future. We also saw that in the municipality of Caroebe, even though it is present in all the schools surveyed, philosophy teaching has been offered basically to comply with the compulsory nature of secondary education, given that the way the subject is being practiced is unlikely to bring about any change in the students' perception of the world.

When you study theories without trying to interpret and understand the concepts you are dealing with, it is difficult for learning to actually take place. Aspis (2004, p. 312) believes that the philosophy teacher needs to be a model, so that, at the same time as presenting the history of philosophy, he/she must also do philosophy, provoking in his/her students the desire to do it too. In this sense, the author compares the philosophy teacher to someone who teaches how to ride a bicycle, since the one who teaches only "[...] shows how, gives support, holds on so as not to fall, activates the spirit, draws attention to the technique of the thing, encourages the search for one's own way of doing it" (ASPIS, 2004, p. 312). For her, a class like this can only be a practical class: "And such a teacher must first of all be a cyclist or a philosopher himself, because otherwise what is he talking about? He who only **talks about** philosophy does not **teach** philosophy" (ASPIS, 2004, p. 312). However, how can teachers with no training in philosophy be expected to cope with the teaching proposed by Aspis?

It was in this sense that we pointed to training by area of knowledge as a possible contribution to overcoming this problem. Even if there is still resistance to its acceptance, it is urgent and necessary, especially in schools that are further away from large urban centers, as is the case with schools in the municipality of Caroebe. We saw that the teachers who graduated from the LEDUCARR faced difficulties in the teacher selection process because they were trained by subject area, showing a certain prejudice towards this type of training. However, when we look at the reality in schools, what we see are teachers with specific training working with various subjects without any qualification, just as a way of completing their workload.

This begs the question: Why this denial? Why so much resistance to formally accepting what has long been common practice in the vast majority of Brazilian schools? We agree with Martinazzo and Cherobini (2005, p. 70-71), who state that overcoming these obstacles will not happen without conflicts, so that:

> Anyone willing to collaborate with this overcoming needs to be prepared to take risks, to break the bonds imposed by the modern Cartesian paradigm, to exchange the certainty and security of modern science for the restlessness and uncertainty of a complex science.

Changing conceptions is necessary, and to do so, raising awareness is still the best way forward, because it is only by being sensitive to the cause that there will be an awareness that it is necessary.

REFERENCES

ARROYO, Miguel Gonzalez. Training of Rural Educators. In: CALDART, R. S.; PEREIRA, I. B; ALENTEJANO, P.; FRIGOTTO, P. (Org.) **Dicionario da Educagao do Campo.** Rio de Janeiro, Sao Paulo: Escola Politecnica de Saude Joaquim Venancio, Expressao Popular, 2012, p.361- 367.

ASPIS, Renata Pereira Lima. The Philosophy Teacher: Teaching Philosophy in High School as a Philosophical Experience. **Caderno Cedes**, Campinas, vol. 24, n. 64, p. 305-320, 2004. Available at: http://www.cedes.unicamp.br.pdf. Accessed on: October 7, 2017.

BRAZIL, **Law No. 13,415, of February 16, 2017.** Brasilia, February 16, 2017.

, MEC. SEB. SECADI. SEPT. CNE. CNEB. **General National Curriculum Guidelines for Basic Education**. Brasilia: MEC, SEB, DICEI, 2013

MEC/ CNE. **National Common Curriculum Base**. Brasilia, 2017.

FAVERO, A. A et al. **The Teaching of Philosophy in Brazil:** a map of current conditions. Caderno Cedes, Campinas, v. 24, n. 64, p. 257-284, 2004. Available at: http://www.cedes.unicamp.br. Accessed on: October 22, 2017.

GABRIEL, Gilvete de Lima; ALBUQUERQUE, Ruti Rodrigues. **The configuration of the Degree in Rural Education in Roraima**: limits and possibilities for the training of basic education teachers. Available at: www.catedraunescoeja.org/GT04/COM/COM001 .pdf. Accessed on: July 28, 2017.

BRAZILIAN INSTITUTE OF GEOGRAPHY AND STATISTICS (IBGE) **Demographic Overview of Caroebe**. Available at: https://cidades.ibge.gov.br/brasil/rr/caroebe/panorama. Accessed on: December 15, 2017.

GALLO, Silvio. **Democratic Governmentality and Philosophy Teaching in Contemporary Brazil.** Cadernos de Pesquisa v.42 n.145 p.48-65, 2012. Available at: http://www.scielo.br/pdf/cp/v42n145/05.pdf. Accessed on: Aug. 22, 2017.

LAGO RODRIGUES, Zita Ana. **The Teaching of Philosophy in Brazil in the context of contemporary educational policies in their legal and paradigmatic determinations**. Educar em Revista, Curitiba, n. 46, p. 69-82, Ed. UFPR, 2012

MARTINAZZO, Celso Jose; CHEROBINI, Ana Lina. **Pedagogy and Complexity:** implications and transdisciplinarity. Revista Contexto e Educagao, Ed. UNIJUI - Ano 20. N° 73/74- p.55 - 72, 2005.

MOLINA, Monica Castagna; ANTUNES-ROCHA, Maria Isabel. Rural **education: history, practices and challenges in the context of educator training policies -** reflections on PRONERA and PROcAMPO. Revista Reflexao e Agao, Santa Cruz do Sul, v.22, n.2, p.220-253, 2014. Available at: http://online.unisc.br/seer/index.php/reflex/index. Accessed on: January 19, 2018.

OLIVEIRA, Cassia Araujo; OLIVEIRA, Andreici Marcela Araujo **O Panorama Curricular do Ensino de Filosofia no Brasil.** Artificios, Revista do Difere - ISSN 2179 6505, v. 2, n.4, 2012. Available at:http://studylibpt.com/doc/809643/o-panorama-curricular-do-ensino-de-filosofia-no-artificios.pdf. Accessed on: July 19, 2017.

RORAIMA, STATE SECRETARIAT FOR EDUCATION AND SPORT (SEED- RR). **Notice PSSCI/SEED/GAB/RR N°002/** - Simplified Selection Process for Temporary Recruitment of Substitute Teachers - Capital/ Interior 2017.

; State Government. **Law No. 892, of January 25, 2013.** "Provides for the creation of the Plan of Positions, Careers and Remunerations for Basic Education Workers in the State of Roraima (PCCREB) and other provisions". Diario Oficial, Boa Vista, n.25, ed. 1960, p.03, 25. Jan. 2013.

TEIXEIRA, Gilson Ruy Monteiro; ALMEIDA, Jerusa da Silva Gongalves; SILVA, Jussara Almeida Midlej. **Philosophy as a subject in secondary education: a** historical approach to its teachability in Brazilian secondary schools. IV International Colloquium "Education and Contemporaneity" Sao Cristovao- SE/Brazil, 2012.

STATE UNIVERSITY OF RORAIMA, **Pedagogical ProJect of the Degree Course in Human Sciences,** Pro-Rectory of Education, Rorainopolis, 2017.

WIKIPEDIA, the free encyclopedia. **List of municipalities in Roraima.** Available at: https://pt.wikipedia.org/wiki/Lista de munic%C3%ADpios de Roraima. Accessed on: 29 Jan. 2018.

AUTHORS

Claudio Sipert

Bachelor's and Licentiate's Degree in Philosophy from the State University of Western Paraná - UNIOESTE, Master's and Doctorate in Philosophy from the State University of Campinas - UNICAMP, with a sandwich period at the Universitat Trier - Germany through the DAAD-Capes program. Professor of Philosophy at the State University of Roraima - UERR. E-mail:claudiosipert@bol.com.br

Cleudicelia Lopes Xavier

Graduated in Field Education, Human and Social Sciences Area, from the Federal University of Roraima - UFRR and Specialist in Fundamentals of Philosophy from the State University of Roraima - UERR. She is a public school teacher in the state of Roraima. E-mail: cleudicelia@hotmail.com

Elemar Kleber Favreto

Bachelor's, Licentiate's and Master's Degree in Philosophy from the State University of Western Paraná - UNIOESTE, Specialist in Municipal Public Management from the State University of Maringa - UEM, Bachelor's Degree in Accounting Sciences from the UNINTER University Center and Licentiate's Degree in Physics from the Institute of Education, Science and Technology of Amazonas - IFAM. Professor of Philosophy at the State University of Roraima - UERR. E-mail:elemar@uerr.edu.br

Marcos Silveira Aranguiz

Bachelor in Theology from the Faculty of Sciences, Education and Theology of the North of Brazil - FACETEN, Specialist in Methodologies of Higher Education and EAD from the Educational Faculty of Lapa - FAEL, Degree in Philosophy and Specialization in Fundamentals of Philosophy from the State University of Roraima - UERR. Teacher in the Private Basic Education Network in the State of Roraima. E-mail:marcosaranguiz@outlook.com

Neusa Wigner Matte

She has a degree in Geography from the Federal University of Roraima - UFRR, a degree in Philosophy from the State University of Roraima - UERR, a degree in Pedagogy from the Faculty of Science, Education and Theology of Northern Brazil - FACETEN and a specialist in Special Education from the UNINTER University Center. Pedagogue and Teacher in the Public Basic Education Network of the State of Roraima. E-mail:wignerneu44@gmail.com

Rafael Parente Ferreira Dias

He has a degree in Philosophy from the Federal University of Rio de Janeiro - UFRJ, a Master's degree in Philosophy from Gama Filho University and a PhD in Religious Sciences from the Federal University of Paraiba - UFPB. Professor of Philosophy at the State University of Roraima - UERR. E-mail: rafael.dias@uerr.edu.br

Renata Viana Serafim

Degree in Philosophy and Specialist in Fundamentals of Philosophy from the State University of Roraima - UERR. Bachelor's Degree in Administration from Faculdade Roraimense de Ensino Superior - FARES. Private school teacher in the state of Roraima. E-mail:renata-viana34@outlook.com

Waldemar Moura Vilhena Junior

BA in Social Sciences with a major in Sociology from the Federal University of Roraima - UFRR, BA in Sociology and MA in Education from the Federal University of Amazonas - UFAM. Professor of the Degree Course in Human Sciences at the State University of Roraima - UERR. E-mail: waldemarvilhena@gmail.com

Printed by Books on Demand GmbH, Norderstedt / Germany